WHAT [

MW01105031

By ELVIRA BELLEGONI

Published by:
ETTA Publishing Company
28605 Lakeshore Blvd.
Willowick, Ohio 44095 U.S.A.

First printing 1999

Printed in the United States of America

ISBN 0-9662542-5-2

i

WHAT DO YOU MEAN I AM FIFTY?

TABLE OF CONTENTS

WHAT DO YOU MEAN I AM FIFTY?

By ELVIRA BELLEGONI

FIRST EDITION

ETTA PUBLISHING COMPANY

I dedicate this book to all the women who have
the courage to change

And

I dedicate my heart to God who gave me the
courage to change.

Elvira Bellegoni

September 1999

Chapter 1: I AM FIFTY

WOW! "Pretend it does not exist and it will go away" did not work.

I woke up this morning and I was fifty. 50? Five-zero? One half century? Five decades? Incredible! How can I be fifty? I never was forty, or even thirty. Maybe I was twenty, I am not sure. Biological age stinks! There is somebody inside who definitely is not fifty, whatever that means.

Really! This is a shock! Am I supposed to feel fifty? Am I supposed to know what to feel like? I remember when, not long ago (ha, ha), I would look at someone my age and think: 'That's old'. I wish my brain had frozen when I thought that! I really am just a cute little girl inside an older container!

I need to look into that mirror. Let's see; yup, those are wrinkles. The skin is sagging a bit, especially around my mouth. It is funny, I think I look like one of those wooden nutcrackers. Did I say it is funny? I think I am losing it! Even the breasts are sagging a bit. Well, I really don't look too bad.

I definitely do not want to look at the backside, my neck is a bit stiff and it would hurt if I turned.
I pinch my skin here and there and wait to see it go back into place...oh-oh.

My dark hair is sprinkled with gray. I used to pluck the gray hair out but I don't do that anymore; the gray hair just keeps on coming back faster than I can pluck it out. Now, if I were a man I would look 'distinguished', but I am not a man. Does the gray bother me? Sure it does. I may be fifty but I am not old! Yes, I will spend the five dollars for hair coloring for a new, youthful me.

So, I am fifty, eh? So what? So what?? Shall I go hide in a closet or under a rug till the day I am no more?

Hell NO!

Heavens YES! I shall live to the fullest.

Sure, easier said than done.

What does that song say? ' ...In the autumn of my years...' Does it mean that from now on it will all be "down hill"? I suppose that as long as the road is straight I should be O.K.!

I know women of all ages, especially those between 40 and 60 and I know some in their 70s and 80s. Sometimes I look at an older woman and try to picture her as a child, then as a teenager, then as a woman. One thing that never seems to change (in my imagining the life span of an older woman) is her eyes. Not the outside but the inside of the eyes, deep inside. Eyes are the most beautiful and amazing part of the human body. Nothing, not even the spoken word, says as much and as clearly as the eyes. I really love eyes and love to look inside them: that is the shortest way to one's soul.

I'll tell you something funny now. (Well, in one minute.) I once had a friend, Helen, about ten years older than me. She was a wonderful friend; she had a good heart and really cared about people. She did not tell me how to be a good person, she showed me. 'Actions speak louder than words' certainly applied to her. She could not gossip about anyone and if she were told some bad things about somebody her reply always was: 'I will pray for him/her, and I will pray for you too.' Once a woman asked her "Why are you going to pray for me too?" My friend answered: "Anyone who needs to say bad things about other people needs prayers". Never again did that woman gossip about someone in front of my friend!

My friend passed away a few years ago from cancer, I miss her. I loved to look into her eyes because her eyes always told me she cared for me, she approved or disapproved of me, and so on. There was no doubt about knowing what she was feeling, the eyes told me.

We used to play golf together at least once a week in the summer time. One day, after playing golf, we were enjoying a soft drink and finding all sort of excuses rationalizing how lousy we both had played golf that day. I suddenly asked her to look at me straight in the eyes and look as deep as she could. I did the same and it was spectacular! I saw specks and specks of light, like brilliant gold, like ever changing facets of diamonds.

I told her I saw a preview of heaven and those lights were probably angels dancing. I asked her what she saw in my eyes and she replied: "You are right. I can really see inside you and what I saw is that a bunch of gray matter is missing! You are a nut!" Well, I guess it did not work for her, and that is O.K.

To this day, her eyes are still so clear in my mind.

Her physical appearance is slowly fading, but not her eyes.

Anyway, getting back on course, I like to try imagining not only how these older women looked through the years, but also what they were saying, how they were saying it, the facial expressions, etc.

At times I do that to myself! I try very hard to think about specific events that happened through my life from early childhood on and then I try to see myself very up close, especially the expression in my eyes and face.

I am going to go off course again!

I tried an experiment once. Another friend had gone on a spiritual weekend and participated in the 'Child Within' program. Part of the program during the weekend was for each participant to close their eyes and go back in time and meet herself when she was a child, and talk to the child. She was so happy from that experience as she had a spiritual awakening and she now knew herself so much better.

She described in some detail what had happened during that weekend and I decided to try to go back and find me when I was a little girl. What a learning experience that was! I loved the little me, so innocent, hopeful, trusting, and fearful too.

I went back to the time I was maybe ten years old. We had just moved into a new apartment. This apartment had one bedroom, one large kitchen, and one bathroom. It even had a small balcony. It was absolutely beautiful compared to the previous apartment. All windows had green shutters and even the balcony had green shutters, from the floor to almost the ceiling. All the floors, including the balcony and the stairway (we lived on the second floor) were beautiful white marble.

(I am going off course while already off course!)

Our apartment building had six apartments, two on each floor. The women took turns, on a weekly basis, to keep the common areas: stairs, walls, and windows clean. They really took pride in this and went as far as putting curtains on those windows and stands with plants at each floor. The stairs looked so clean and so white and smelled so good.

My family, back then, consisted of my mother, father, and two brothers and this apartment was a beautiful castle!

To carry out my meeting with the little me I went to a park which was peaceful, with trees, flowers, fresh cut grass, and a lake just a few yards away. It was a picture-perfect place; peace would enter my heart as I would walk in.

I had been going to this place on a regular basis, especially when I needed some serenity. I have been calling it 'place', but it is a beautiful garden that belongs to St. Joseph Christian Life Center. Here you find gardens 'galore'. There are the Stations of the Cross and each station is adorned with plants and flower plants. There are many other flower gardens throughout and the birds and the squirrels are a joy to hear and watch.

I sat down on the grass, my back and head resting against a large tree. No one was around as it was rather early in the morning. I closed my eyes and I went to meet the little girl in the new apartment.

It took a while before I could really concentrate; my mind free of anything else.

The little me was cleaning small debris from the floor left by the painting of the walls. She was wearing a nice little outfit; blue matching pants and top. Her hair was long, shiny, and parted in the middle. It was strange to realize that I did not even introduce myself; we just started talking as if we always had been talking. She was so happy and proud of the apartment and she promised to keep it clean every day. She told me about the previous apartment, how bad it was. She had been praying that her family would get a better apartment, especially because she wanted to see her mother happy.

It was even stranger when, at a point, I realized we were no longer in the apartment, but she was sitting next to me under the tree.

We talked for what seemed to be a very long time, we held hands, we hugged, and I cried for most of this time. There were sad stories she told me and she told me of her fears. I felt her pain and I felt her fear. I told her that I knew she would be O.K. because God loved her so much and I knew there would always be an angel walking with her. She believed me and she also told me that she knew I too, would be watching over her. We hugged once more.

It was at this moment that I was brought back to 'reality' by two squirrels complaining very loudly that I better move from their tree.

Although it seemed that we talked for a very long

time, I guessed it was for maybe fifteen minutes. It was a wonderful experience and a sad one as well. I knew the past could not be undone.

It took me a while before I was able to leave. I went over and over again my meeting with the little me. I could not figure out how we went from her apartment to under the tree.

To this day I have not been able to go back again. Whenever the thought comes into my mind I realize that I am not ready yet for another encounter.

I will be going to that weekend program; though today I am not ready for it, I know I will need to be with the little me again.

A note of caution: I related my experience to one of this weekend program's presenters and I was told not to do it again alone because without guidance I could have hurt myself deeply emotionally.

O.K., time that we go back on course.

How was my life? Did I live a good and meaningful life?

I always thought that through the course of life I would have known true love, I would have been rich, I would have been famous, I would have been known for my beauty...

The word 'would' stinks too. Actually, the words 'would', 'could', and 'should' have been part of my vocabulary for so long; no wonder I have a hard time thinking in terms of biological aging. The sentences that begin with 'I should have', 'I could have', 'I would have' have been part of my 'lingo' for so long I am surprised I don't feel like one hundred instead of fifty!

I have read the definition of 'regrets' in the dictionary...I better be careful.

I have to do some reviewing of my life because I really don't know if I ever had a great love, or was rich, or was famous, or had great beauty....

Maybe I did - and maybe I have.

Let's leave love for last, I don't want to get mushy just yet.

Chapter 2: RICH

How do I define the word rich? Millions and billions and zillions of dollars? The most expensive cars, maids and butlers, a jet to work? Would all that make me rich? Would it be enough?

While I am on the subject I better check to see how much cash I have in my wallet. The newspaper carrier is coming this morning and I'll need fifteen dollars and that includes the tip. Yes, I have enough.

Enough: that is a novel concept! I have enough; is that being rich?

I remember: I definitely know I was fifteen! Fifteen years old; that is, thirty five years ago! This is worthy of another WOW. So, here is how it was. There was mom, dad, and three brothers.

The oldest brother four years older than me, and the brothers are each ten years apart, so let see, if I am fifty then they are fifty four, forty four, and thirty four.

I sure have a hard time thinking about them in terms of the biological age, especially the baby brother, he is still a baby! The 'baby' has a ten-year-old son....

I am beginning to feel weird.

Anyway, let me tell you something about me. I was born and raised in Italy in such a beautiful town: Carrara, the city of the most magnificent marble. Ah, those hills. I'll postpone telling you about my hometown till later.

Father was a bricklayer. In the summertime it was 'feast' and in the wintertime it was 'famine'. Dad worked only if it was not raining (much) and if it was not very cold as all the work he did was outside.

In the summertime we would put 'stuff' away for the winter months, mostly non-perishable foods.

I remember when we bought a refrigerator/freezer: what an absolute luxury! You should have seen mother: better than a busy bee, better than a working ant! All the foods she prepared and put in the freezer! She was so happy! She used to say: "We won't starve -- unless 'they' shut off the electricity!" and she would laugh.

Yes, we were pretty good 'squirrels' at storing necessities for the lean times.

(I read this part of the book to my mother. She told me: "All I have done for you and you are calling me an insect? Just remember that bees sting!" – She does have a good sense of humor.)

I do remember some of the 'lean' times. It was rather sad to see mom and dad worry so much about money. I certainly did not help to make them feel better, I remember I did not like to wear used cloths or play with used toys, and I would say so.

I would ask for things and I could not understand why I could not have them. I never stopped long enough to think.

I remember that in one year we were 'kicked out' from two apartments because we could not pay the rent. We all felt humiliated, especially because the neighbors knew what was happening.

There was bickering at home now and it always had to do with money, or the lack of it.

I remember well this particularly sad and worrisome time in our family when we also had to accept charity. I do remember that charity. They delivered so much food and clothes one time that is was better than our best Christmas in a long time.

Every other week mother and I would walk about five miles (each way) to go pick up food at that charity. We could not afford the bus fare, so we had to walk. Going was not that bad, but coming back was so tiring. Both mother and I would carry two or three bags filled with food. Mother would have to stop frequently, her eyes looking so tired, her hands so red and swollen from the handles of the bags.

Once home we would put everything on the kitchen table and go lay down in bed for about one hour. Before dozing off mother would say: "Don't forget to thank God. For two more weeks you won't starve. You will keep that beautiful double chin." She would giggle and fall asleep.

That break would give us enough energy to start unpacking the food and then packing it up again for storage. If there was any perishable food we would cook it right away, wait for it to cool, and then we would package it and put it in the freezer. She would carefully label everything: a good description of the content and the date. I remember one time opening the freezer and pulling out those delicious cookies. There were two labels on the package: one to describe the content and the other read 'Elvira, keep your paws off.'

Both mother and father felt somewhat humiliated about accepting charity, and I did hear father once tell mother that he was a failure. Poor dad.

How selfish I was. I could only worry about me; about what I had or did not have. How much less anguish and sadness would my parents have been spared if I were less selfish, more understanding, and more loving?

Now for a reality check.

Let me think real hard. Did I ever go to bed hungry, with an empty belly? Very interesting: I cannot think of a single time I went to bed hungry.

I am giggling now as I am going through pictures of when I was a baby and a young girl: look at that double chin! I really had a double chin! I definitely never went to bed hungry.

I am beginning to feel rich. Never went to bed hungry and always had nice, clean clothes to wear.

Did your mom use to tell you: "Always wear clean clothes just in case you get in an accident"? What kind of thinking is that? Oh, well.

Clothes

I am a 'clothes-horse'. I have more clothes in the closet that I could possibly ever wear out. Why do I have so many clothes? And why do I have some clothes that are years old and have been worn just once or twice?

Talking about old clothes – I have a mini skirt which is about thirty years old. It looks almost like a tapestry design and the cloth is very strong (maybe it was tapestry!) I can still wear it (if I suck in air and stop breathing) but I cannot move. If I were to try to sit down, it would certainly split. I weigh just about the same as I did back then, but now I am experiencing the 'funnel' effect! If you don't know what that is, it is when the top gets smaller and the bottom larger.

I brought this skirt with me from Italy, promising myself I would never throw it out. Evidently, this skirt has a deep meaning to me, but: I cannot remember what it is! This is terrible! Now I definitely have to keep it, at least until I remember why I wanted to keep it in the first place. (Do you think my forgetting has anything to do with being fifty?)

I have to stop now to tell you something that happened just the other day that made me feel ashamed of myself, mostly because I keep on realizing that I am very selfish.

I was in a store and on my way to the photo counter I walked by the children's clothes section. Two women were holding up little girls' outfits and talking to each other. The topic of the conversation was the possibility that the store would let one of the women put the outfit she was holding on 'layaway'. Both women looked in their late twenties, very pretty but unkept, no make-up, no jewelry, no nice clothes. I kept on going, but on my way back I got curious. I stopped at the girls' clothes section and looked at the price of the outfit, twenty-two dollars! I felt so bad! That woman did not have twenty-two dollars to buy that outfit! How many twenty-two dollars have I wasted? I felt so bad for her but I also felt bad for myself as once again I was taking things for granted, once again I forgot where I came from.

Let us get back to my clothes. Yes, look at this

pretty little green dress, when was the last time I wore it? I can't remember. I better start wearing it or the moths might get indigestion.

Oh, I remember back then: way back then. How proud I was! I know I was the prettiest girl! That dress that mom made for me for my first communion. It was so beautiful. I can still see myself, I can still feel the happiness and pride. Mom made that dress for me. I wasn't planning on getting this mushy, but my mom was really good (that's because she is MY mom! -- Do I sound like I am fifty years old to you?) She would sew so many beautiful things, not just clothes.

Those curtains she made. She cut and sewed the curtains, then she crocheted the most beautiful white roses, complete with stems and leaves, and sewed them on the curtains. Oh yes, those curtains were the talk of the town; and my mom made them.

These feelings, I feel like a happy child and I feel richer by the minute.

I am fifty? Don't bet on it.

How long has it been since I thought about my communion dress, about those curtains? Too long, way too long. This is what makes me feel old: not remembering beautiful things. 'Young at heart': I am just beginning to get the message!

I am still browsing through pictures of my youth; I always wore pretty and clean clothes.

In my early teens I always tried to look older by wearing 'adult' clothes instead of teenager clothes. I wanted to look elegant and older. Poor mom, I was such a little troublemaker. I remember the times I 'stole' her stockings, her high-heel shoes, and her lipstick – I always got caught! I also 'stole' her bra and was wearing it but I had 'nothing' to put into it! I think I got a spanking once. Such a rush to grow up. Now things are the opposite! Go figure.

Oh my! What I am remembering now! The wooden ball mother used to mend socks with! She used to mend stockings too. That DOES sound like ancient history!

Yes, I never lacked for food or clothes or a roof over my head yet, I did do a lot of complaining. At times I even was ashamed of what I had or did not have and I was a liar. I thought I had so little that I always exaggerated and lied about what I had or did not have.

Selfishness? Definitely!

Ignorance? Absolutely!

I just remembered something else. My first car. Dear Lord, didn't I feel rich and important? I sure did. My first car, a FIAT 600, a mini-mini car which was falling apart. It did not have working brakes and to stop I had to use the hand brakes! To stop the car, once, I actually opened the car door and put my foot down to the ground. Don't you believe me? It is the truth. There were quite a few things that were wrong with that car! I seem to recall that I paid about 10 dollars for it. Yes, ten dollars which had taken me 'forever' to save. How long did it last? Probably about six or nine months, I don't really remember. I also recall, during those six or nine months, not having enough money to buy gas when the tank was empty. I also remember that, when I had gas, I would go for drives just so that people would see me driving my car! I was broke but any chances I got I would waste gas money to show off, to make you think I had something. I felt so important driving MY car to my jobs.

My jobs...we need to stop here, or I am afraid I might forget to tell you about this particular job!

The 'self employed typist'.

This is a job I will remember forever! Although I did not know it back then, this job gives meaning to the saying 'where there is a will there is a way'. It has taught me courage, perseverance, and humility.

I still had an elementary education at that time and the most 'sophisticated' job I had had up to that point was selling encyclopedias. Actually, I should say 'trying' to sell encyclopedias, as in the span of three months I sold three encyclopedias: one to a 'real' customer, one to a relative (after proper begging), and one to myself!

My father had just passed away and no income was coming into our household. Something had to be done. A friend of mine had obtained a good job as a typist and so I decided that if she could do that so could I. (She studied to be a typist I did not.) I knew I could not go look for a job as an employee; I neither had the education nor the experience to do anything. Therefore, I did the next best thing: I put an ad in the local paper making myself available as an independent typist.

By now you might be asking yourself: "Well, what

is so special about that?" "Not much" is the answer, except that up to that point not only I did not know how to type, but I also had never even been close to a typewriter!

I did get my first job, typing contracts for an attorney. I went to the attorney's office, got all the papers and promised that the typed contracts would be delivered within two weeks. We also agreed on my 'billing rates' (I had no clue about how that was done! I am sure I knew nothing about billing rates.)

So, now I had the job, which meant three things needed to be done:

1. Buy a typewriter,
2. Learn how to type, and
3. Do the job.

(I know that the saying 'more courage than brains' was developed in my honor.)

I went to buy a typewriter and, though I remember very little about the buying process, I did buy an Olivetti 32 manual typewriter. (It is a very small typewriter, probably the size of a laptop computer.)

The next five or six days were spent almost entirely in learning how to type. I would type whenever I had the chance and especially at night, after everyone had gone to sleep. Within two weeks the work was delivered: correct and on time!

I was so proud of myself. I really learned a new skill well enough that I received a second job from the same attorney. Later on I learned that what would take me an entire day to type would take someone else (skilled at typing) just a couple of hours. That was O.K. though, I wanted to learn a new skill and I did it. I wanted (and really needed) to bring money in the house and I did.

A year later I did take a course on stenography and typing and received a diploma. I don't know what happened to that diploma. I was so proud of it and I lost it!

That typewriter is today one of my most prized possessions. It sits inside it original carrier on my desk, in my office. It is a good reminder that hard work and perseverance have their own rewards.

At that time I really did not have the knowledge, wisdom, or the time to assess the implications of this job. How very beneficial this experience would be in shaping my character, in giving me strength and hope, and in knowing that I could succeed in just about anything if I really tried.

By the way, today I still type except I only use two fingers. Why? I don't know. I guess I forgot how to use ten fingers or my fingers got lazy.

As the years passed material things came to be so important, they become the pursuit of happiness.

I wanted a house: I got it and it was not enough.

I wanted 'tons' of clothes: I got them and they were not enough.

I wanted money, jewelry, and I wanted to travel: I got them all and they were not enough.

I wanted, and I wanted, and I wanted: I got what I wanted and I still wanted and I still could not fill the deep void.

What a fool I was. The riches of material things came, and the riches of the heart went. I now know that I was the poorest when I was the richest: poorest in spirit and in happiness. The bigger the pot of gold, the bigger the hole in my soul.

When did I realize that I always was rich? When did I realize I had gone astray? The day came and I will tell you about it later.

Would you like to know something about my hometown now? (You better say yes because I am going to tell you anyway.)

I grew up in Carrara. Carrara is in Tuscany; about twenty miles from the leaning tower of Pisa, and fifty miles from Florence to the east and about sixty miles from the French Riviera to the West. I close my eyes and I see my hometown. I see the boulevard that spans from the mountains to the sea. From the mountains to the sea is only about 20 miles.

Let's start with the mountains, those are the marble quarries which give the beautiful warm pure white marble. That is the marble Michelangelo used to carve his statues.

Have you ever read the book 'The Agony and the Ecstasy'? Or watched the movie? If you saw the movie you saw Carrara, if you read the book you felt Carrara.

Carrara is hugged on the back by the quarries and as you come down toward the sea you will find

Fossola and Avenza; two small, clean, and pretty towns. The towns are caressed by hills, hills filled with vineyards and olive trees. Further south is Marina di Carrara, so pretty, clean, and simple.

The beaches are renowned all over Europe, the sand is fine and gentle. Tourists, especially from Germany, start arriving in early spring and keep coming until late in the autumn.

Dear God, so much beauty and I never saw it! Blind: how blind I was and for so long! I wanted to get away from Carrara real bad. I blamed the town for my miseries. The town had nothing to do with my miseries, but I certainly did!

It is true that it is much easier to blame somebody, or something, rather than to be honest with one's self.

Am I rich? Yes, without a shadow of a doubt, I am rich. Even if I did not have a penny today, I would still tell you that I am rich. Yes, now I know that I have always been rich. Can you understand this?

Chapter 3: FAMOUS

I now think that if I want to be 'famous' as the rest of the world might interpret this word, I should have my head checked, not once but twice. I actually had the gull to think that I could easily be a Sofia Loren, a Florence Nightingale, etc., etc. I spent so much time dreaming about being that famous actress, nurse, and so on, that it is a miracle I actually was able to do anything.

What does it mean to be famous? Of course, if you are dollar-rich you are automatically famous. It seems to me though that it is the dollar that is famous, not the person that has it. Nowadays, there is a tendency to call a person 'famous' if that person makes the national news--good or bad! (Hell, some of the 'bad news' makers have even written best sellers!)

That reminds me about what one local paper has done. For close to a week the paper publicized an interview, which would be printed in the Sunday paper. They devoted a few pages to that interview: an interview with a 'cop killer'! Why make the bad famous? (I no longer subscribe to that paper.)

Enough, I sound like I know it all and I can judge anything or anyone.

Let me look at me: am I famous? Yes, yes, yes, I am.

Do you know that when I was fifteen years old I wrote a poem about my father who had just passed away and it was published in the local paper?

Did I get paid for it? No.

Did anyone ask me to write more poems? No.

Did people know whom I was when they saw me go by? No.

Still I say I was (and am) famous. Why? Oh, come on, can't you guess? It is the heart! I suppose I should explain this better. You see I had done something good. My mother told me so. My mother told me I was so smart.

My mother also told me that my father would be so proud of me. Well, mushy time is coming. First I want you to read the poem I wrote:

You are gone...I miss you.

It took your death to make me know.
Such a strict man of very few words.
What are words when I failed to look into your eyes?
I resented you, when did you tell me you loved me last?
Why did I hide my love for you from you?
How did I long for a hug.
Why did I shun you?

You are gone...I miss you.

I never understood you, I never understood your pain.
Now you are gone, now I understand.
I know you loved me, I know you wanted to love me more.
The flower on your tomb will last but one day.
My sorrow will last for how long?
Forgive me God, forgive me daddy.

You are gone...I miss you.

After my father was taken ill with cancer I took it upon myself (no victim here--no one asked me) to become the breadwinner of the family. Of course I had no skills (before the self-employed typist) but I pretended I did and I somehow managed. At one time I had six part-time jobs and could do none well. My jobs ranged from working in a dry cleaners shop to selling encyclopedias (that is a real laugh; at that time I had an elementary school education, but I was selling encyclopedias!).

I actually liked what I was doing and wanted to learn more about it, but I also was beginning to resent my father. I resented him because I was in such a predicament and I resented him because I thought he did not love me enough as he did not show much affection. (Remember when I talked about the eyes? If I asked my father a question and expected a 'yes' or a 'no' as an answer, I would look into his eyes and he did not have to utter a word – I would know what the answer was.)

The morning of my father's last trip to the hospital (thinking all his children were asleep) I heard him tell my mother: "This is the last time I see my children. I love them so much", and then I heard him sobbing. It was like a big rock had fallen on my head! An instantaneous horrible headache, panic that took my breath away, guilt, guilt, guilt. I cried and I prayed and I asked God to cure him.

Up to that point, although I was told he had cancer, it really had not sunk in that my father was a dying man. I was too busy criticizing him, not believing he was ill, and just feeling sorry for myself.

Now I knew, it was sinking in, and I was sinking in pain. I made a promise to my father that day, while I was in my bed and he was going to the hospital to die: 'I will make you proud of me, dad.'

Publishing that poem made me famous. I knew that now my father knew I really loved him and that I wrote that poem to show my love for him.

So, do you understand now? I was as famous as famous can be!

There are so many wonderful things that happened to me that made me feel so famous, things that to the material world mean very little but to the spiritual world they heal the soul.

As I grew up and as the material world became all so important so did the need to achieve status in the community. I did work hard, acquired many material things, and accomplished much.

For a while it was almost as if I was in a frenzy: nothing, absolutely nothing was more important than obtaining 'status' within the community. I would write and publish articles, give seminars, volunteer for so many business organizations, and on, and on. Being recognized was so important and so consuming.

When I finally looked back I saw a list of 'I should have', 'I could have', 'I would have' without end. Did I work hard at making people around me happy? No. What would happen to the material things if I had become ill? Were these amongst my accomplishments:

Take time for my loved ones? No.

Take time to smile to a passerby? No.

Take time to listen to someone's problems, fears, hopes? No.

What happened? Where is the child? I will tell you later.

Am I famous? Today yes. When my mind and my heart resemble the heart and the mind of when I wrote my father's poem, yes, indeed I am famous.

Chapter 4: BEAUTY

I was Miss America once....then I woke up!

Beautiful: what does the word mean? We use the word 'beautiful' to describe people, cars, pets, and anything else in between. I am going to look it up in the dictionary. Beautiful: it is something that brings pleasure to the senses when looked at. What a waste! Can you see the soul of a person?

If you are catholic, let me ask you a question: the Virgin Mary stood by as her son was put to death, she did not put up a struggle. How beautiful, do you suppose, was she to look at? But the Virgin Mary was, is, and will be to the end of all times the most beautiful woman that ever lived.

How beautiful was MLK? But HE WAS a most beautiful man.

Let me give you another example. I was a witness to this. In church I happened to notice a young boy, Mark, maybe 10 years old, looking at another boy. The other boy was in a wheelchair, in the aisle. I could see Mark's sadness as he watched people exiting the church without even looking at the boy. Mark got up and went to the handicapped boy. He touched him in the shoulder, he smiled at him, shook hands with him, and started talking to him.

How beautiful can beautiful be?

Do you see where I am going? The outside beauty comes and goes, the beauty inside is everlasting.

Well, I guess you did not know I was such a philosopher, right?

Coming back down to earth I need to tell you that to the world outside I probably look 'average', pretty you might say. I take care of myself; a bit of make up (though I still don't know how to put make up on!), nice clothes, I watch what I eat and, in the overall, I try to appear the best I can be. Nothing wrong with that.

How many times was I told that I was beautiful? A few times, mostly by family and friends.

Family and friends: aren't they the most important people in our lives? It should be so; however, we usually appear our best for strangers and not for our loved ones, isn't that right? We spend hours 'beautifying' ourselves to go to a party and as soon as we are home it is 'rags'. It doesn't make much sense but that is how it usually is. What would happen if one day we got up and spent a great deal of time making ourselves look beautiful to stay home with our loved ones? We probably would cause some heart attacks!

(Do I know how to preach or what?).

How many times have I been told I was a beautiful person? A few times.

So what is beauty to me? To TRY to be good and to do good, that is beautiful.

Now I'll tell you a secret on how to achieve real beauty: Do something nice for somebody without that 'somebody' finding out who did the good deed. Do you think that is easy to do? Absolutely not! (Especially when *selfishness* is your middle name. I know it is mine!)

You have to do it right, and to do it right it must be 'big' to you. For example, you have that very nice gift you bought for yourself. You had to save and to plan. Here is what you do: give it away to someone you know really needs it and remember this very well: you must remain anonymous and if confronted you have to deny it.

Let me give you another example: you just did your budget for the coming month and you are worried because it looks like you'll only have one hundred dollars left: give fifty dollars away.

This is hard to do. It is very easy to donate fifty dollars when you know you absolutely don't need it. As a matter of fact, it is so easy that it does not mean anything.

Give what you really want for yourself and DON'T LOOK BACK -- If you can do that you will be and you will feel beautiful.

I have to tell you something though, just in case you think I am a wingless angel. Someone had suggested I do what I told you to do and I did it and it was worth nothing, zilch, de nada. Why? Because after I performed my good deed I wanted that person to know that it was me that did such a wonderful thing, and when that person did not come to that conclusion I really felt hurt, insulted, and just plain mad. After all, who else but me would do such a wonderful deed? (Modesty: did I spell it right?) It took quite a few trials before the day came that I gave and did not look back and I sincerely prayed for that person to get all that was needed.

I'll tell you something else that really makes me feel 'oh so good' and beautiful.

Go into a store and look for a mother with a child. See what goes on and if you feel good about both of them, buy the child the toy, outfit, or whatever it is that mother says she cannot buy. Take it to the cashier, pay for it, and have someone give the gift and the cashier's receipt to the child. In the meantime disappear. You cannot run the risk of having either the mother, or the child, or the one who delivered the gift spot you. Try this with a pure heart and feel the beauty, almost euphoria!

(When I do these 'stunts' I strategically park my car so that I can see the exit fairly well. I love to see them come out still talking and laughing about the surprise present the child received. I really get true joy from these experiences.)

If you can do this, you would have done something good, but that is only half of the story, the other half is that you probably would have made someone very happy. In so doing, you might even have helped someone restore her/his faith in the human race.

When you do something nice for somebody in anonymity, and you do it with a good and pure heart (expecting nothing in return) you will get back that goodness ten fold!

Now, read this very carefully:

All the good deeds I have done in the past are now worth close to nothing because I have so disclosed how 'wonderful' I am. What this means is that I just have to start all over. It is all right; I have the rest of my life to do 'good'.

Chapter 5: LOVE

I don't watch too much television or go to the movies, thank heavens! I am a romantic at heart. I cry easily when I watch movies (especially the old ones) about love between a man and a woman, but even more so about the non-romantic love.

I believe in 'real' love. Do I know what 'real' love is? Probably not.

My heart is capable of loving and I have loved; I just am not sure of what makes a love a 'real' love. I experienced 'puppy' love, the first innocent love; I experienced the 'adult' love, the love between a man and a woman, and I experienced the greatest love of all: the love of God.

Do you remember that somewhere in the book I told you that I fantasized quite a bit? In my teens I used to 'fall in love' with whomever was the current 'star', an actor or singer. I would spend hours fantasizing. My fantasies always ran from when we met to when my 'star' would ask me to marry him, then I would get bored and move on to another fantasy.

When I was in my mid teens I fell in love with the boy 'next door'. He was one or two years older than me, very nice looking, dark hair and eyes, slim and tall. We started dating and we had a good time together. We would see each other every day for one hour or so, and then on Sundays we usually spent the afternoon together. I remember our long walks to the beach and on the beach. We would go swimming and then we would run under the pine trees. We would collect pinecones and, from our hidden spot, throw them at people. We would laugh so hard. We would kiss gently and hold hands. It was a sweet, simple, and innocent love. I don't know how long it lasted or why it stopped.

My first love and I hardly remember it! I do have good feelings about it, though.

Soon after my first love something happened that is not good, not good at all. It made my life miserable for a very long time. That was the worst time of my young life. I was raped.

He was a friend of the family, a married man with children almost as old as me. I always had good feelings for him, as if he were a member of my family, and I never saw it coming. I was raped and it was ugly. I had lost my virginity, the virginity that I would have saved for the one who one day was to become my husband. I lost it in a moment of terror, of shame, of guilt. The shame was very bad for a long time. I felt I no longer was worthy of any love, from anybody: I was 'dirty'.

I never said a word to anybody; how could I? Who would have believed me? Moreover, if I had told my parents and they would have believed me, they would have killed him. I kept this dark secret inside me for a very long time. Things were a bit different back then, when I was growing up. Sex was to be left for married people and one just did not talk about it.

Many years have passed since then and I have been able to forgive the rapist. It certainly was not easy. Although it only happened once, for years I lived in fear and in shame. I hated him and wished I could have done him bodily harm. Somehow I also had been blaming myself for what had happened, and before I could forgive him I had to forgive myself.

I had to forgive myself not because I had done something wrong, but for thinking that I could have caused that accident and for thinking that I was worth less as a person because of what had happened.

I am sorry if I saddened you, but I needed to talk about this.

I married when I was twenty-one and after nineteen and one half years of marriage I was divorced. I had many good years with him and I am very grateful for all the goodness he put into my life. The good times certainly outweigh the bad times, but I still divorced him. If you think I am nuts (and you are not alone) for having divorced him, don't think so. I needed to do what I did to find myself and to find my God.

It was a friendly divorce and never were harsh words exchanged. He was rather baffled, as he could not understand why I wanted a divorce. I could not explain it very well either; I knew it had to be done, I needed to be on my own, but I could not really find the words to fully explain why.

I did feel bad about causing him pain and a drastic change in his lifestyle, in his way of living. I felt sorrow and I felt guilt.

I chose to leave him everything: what was his, what was ours, and what was mine. I asked him if I could have enough money for a down payment on a house, and that is all I asked for. I have never regretted what I did and how I did it. I was fair to him and he knew that.

I have to tell you that we are good friends today and if I ever needed anything I know he would be there for me, and he knows I would be there for him.

I also have to tell you that to love somebody you don't need to be with that somebody. I love my ex-husband very much, almost as much as when he was my husband, but I had to leave none-the-less.

Have you ever made a decision for which you really, deep down, cannot explain why you made it, but you HAD to make it? Think about it and if your answer is yes, maybe you will understand me better.

Have I known true love? What I think is true love? Yes, I have. My ex-husband has allowed me to know true love. The love between two human beings. I had to lose that love to find another true love, a love that allows me and wants me to be the best I can be, a love that will endure eternity, a love that is based on purity: the love of God.

Chapter 6: THE LOVE OF GOD

I was born and raised catholic. My family went to church once a week and on major holy days. My parents were not very religious and did not impose religion on their children. After I completed elementary school my parents decided that I should not continue my schooling, as there was not enough money to pay for two schooling. My eldest brother had to continue his education and, besides, my parents did not see a need for me to continue my education: 'you'll get married and will have to stay home, so you don't need to go to school.'

I really did not like their decision, not a bit. I wanted to go to school; I liked to go to school and I liked to study. This was unfair!

Somewhere I read or heard that if I became a nun all my education, as much as I wanted would be paid in full. I started going to church every day. I prayed every day and I studied religion as much as I could. I would borrow books from the church and I would spend time with the priest talking religion. All this brought me close to God and I sincerely believe I loved God and His teachings; however, there was an ulterior motive to my wanting to become a nun: I wanted to go to school, not necessarily to lead a religious life. The result was, none-the-less, that I obtained a new understanding and renewed love for God.

The time came that I had to tell my mother I wanted to become a nun. She did not like the idea at all, so much so that I was forbidden from going to church by myself.

That was it! I was not going to become a nun, or worse yet, get an education. Slowly but surely I abandoned the idea of becoming a nun and it did not take me long to also forget about God.

Life continued but somehow I knew I was going to go back to God; I had unfinished business and one day it would be finished.

All through life I never forgot this unfinished business. The opportunities to go back to church were not there until about eight years ago.

About eight years ago, divorced, I was living alone and my only companions were a 'bunch' of cats who clearly believed I was their pet. (I absolutely love cats and I will tell you about them later). My job was all right and the fear that I would not be able to make it on my own had finally (almost) disappeared.

A few years before that I had joined a twelve-step program. God, His mercy and love, are part of the foundations of this program and that is how, slowly, I started getting close to God again. By now I had irrefutable proof that God exists and He exists to make the world a better place. He exists to bring peace to troubled hearts, like mine.

My heart had been troubled for a while now. I was finally on my own but nothing had really changed. I did not know how to change, or, for that matter, what to change. My soul was screaming for spirituality but I did not know how to find it, where to look for it.

I had a decent home, a nice car, a 'few' jobs, my beloved kitties, and my basic necessities were taken care of. Now what?

I am not sure how my spiritual journey started, but it did. The twelve steps program has a prayer, the Serenity Prayer:

'God grant me the serenity to accept the things I can not change,

Courage to change the things I can, and

The wisdom to know the difference.'

I needed to know what to change and I needed to know how to change it.

My professional life was good, I had worked very hard at it, but now I realized it was just a job. I had also been teaching at local colleges for many years and, although I have always loved to teach, the material I was teaching had become somewhat dry, boring. I also felt as if I did not belong, or, put another way, I was not where I really belonged.

I still had not gone back to church and could not bring myself to going.

There was something I always enjoyed doing, and that was writing. The poem for my father was the first time I wrote something and it brought some peace through the years when I would recite the poem. In my professional career I did write many articles which were published in local and in national magazines; however, although I was proud of these accomplishments, they did not bring any peace.

I definitely knew I needed God in my life, but I needed to do things which would bring me close to Him.

At about this time I read a book 'Do What You Love, the Money Will Follow' (by Marsha Sinetar, Dell Publishing.) That book gave me *the courage to change the things I can.*

How did I find that book?

I was a volunteer in a Christian bookstore (I still am a volunteer there today) and that day I was troubled, almost agitated. Nothing was really wrong and that day had gone rather smoothly. I even had the time for a nice walk in the flower garden. I could not understand why I was feeling so. The fact that no customers were coming in the bookstore did not help either, as I was also bored. Again, I started telling myself I was not doing what I was really meant to do in life; however, the mortgage must be paid every month! Fear of financial insecurity and besides, why 'fix something that is not broken'?

I said a little prayer: "I am troubled my God, I

don't know why. Please show me the way." Then, something happened.

How did I know to go to that particular shelf and pull out the book on the very bottom and start reading it right on the spot? How the books were stacked neither the title nor anything else about this book could be seen. It is as if I was being pushed there. Is this a 'mystery'? I really do not believe so. I think (actually, I know) I listened and was willing to let Him help me.

Chapter 7: WHAT HAPPENED

That evening, at home, I read most of the book. I know I did not read every single word; my eyes were moving faster than my ability to read every word. At one point I put the book down and went in front of the mirror. I looked at my face, almost as if I was looking to a stranger. Then I looked into my eyes and I asked myself: 'Do you love God enough to trust Him, to have faith in Him?' My eyes swelled with tears and I realized I had *the courage to change the things I could change* and I was going to do it!

It was very late, probably two in the morning, but I felt quite awake and refreshed. I went into my little office, sat down with a nice cup of leftover coffee (warmed up in the microwave), and started writing:

This is what I need to do:

1. *Go back to church,*

2. *Find out if you want to pursue religion further,*

3. Start writing,

*4. Down size your business – keep only
   the clients you feel good about,*

*5. Keep teaching but teach what you like
   also, like Italian!*

*6. Thank God everyday for everything you
   have,*

7. Be content.

I put the pen down and read what I wrote. I said a little prayer:

'Take my hand and guide me God, I need you.'

Then I went to bed and I know there must have been angels dancing around me. I felt so happy, protected, unafraid, and serene. I slept like a baby.

Of the seven items listed above do you know how many have been accomplished? SEVEN.

Mind you, miracles did not happen. (Actually, I am a nice miracle.) The money did not start pouring in, as a matter of fact, I work harder than I ever did

and make less money, and IT IS EVERYTHING I
HOPED FOR.

I want to go through the seven items with you,
one by one.

1. *Go back to church.*

I went back to church. The first time I felt like a lost puppy. I could not remember a single prayer. In church I would feel somewhat embarrassed: parishioners knew all the prayers, they knew what to say to celebrate mass, they would sing, and do things. I could do nothing except watch, as I knew nothing. I was amazed as to how much I had forgotten about religion. Just about everything I had learned I had forgotten. It got easier and eventually I felt rather comfortable in church.

I hopped around until I found one church that I truly felt comfortable with; that is, with both the church and its people. I call it 'my real home.' I had to re-learn religion, the meanings, songs, and prayers too. I started volunteering in various capacities and the more I volunteered the more I learned, the more I felt like I really belonged.

My favorite task is that of Eucharistic Minister. It brings me so close to God, and I feel so privileged to be part of such a blessed service.

The words 'this is my body', 'this is my blood' remind me every single time of how much He loves me. Sometimes I do feel guilty knowing that He loves me so much though I do not deserve His love.

I have also developed a few good friendships and these are certainly a greater payback than I ever imagined.

2. Find out if you want to pursue religion further.

I really jumped into religion with 'both feet' so to speak. When I had started going back to church I felt like a lost puppy', now I feel comfortable with everything and my heart is filled with love for God.

I started going to church even when there was no mass. I would go just to be in His company, in His house, to listen to Him and to talk to Him.

I explored the possibility of the vocation of sisterhood. I had attended some spiritual workshops presented by nuns, and through my church I had met and befriended some nuns. I felt good in their company, I liked their view of life, of God, of people. They looked serene, at peace with themselves (and I certainly wanted that.)

I decided to attend a weekend about vocations. I did talk with priests and nuns and gathered as much information as I could. I spent much time in meditation, listening to God. Much time was also spent in determining what I had and what I was willing to surrender.

A week later I had made the decision that

sisterhood was not a vocation I intended pursuing. I felt good with that decision and at peace. I felt very good especially because I knew my love for God would not change.

By the way: I am not a 'bible thumper'. I have come to love religion and I feel very comfortable in church; however, I am not suggesting that you should also become religious and start going to church. 'To each its own' – whatever works. The only thing I would ask of you is this: allow God to love you.

3. *Start writing.*

I wrote my first book. It was not hard to do as it was based upon material I had taught as well as practiced in my business. I sent it to ten publishers and I received ten rejections! (What do they know, anyway!) Of course, I had been thinking that all ten would accept it and actually would beg me to publish my book with them. What an awakening! (Since then I have learned that even very famous authors have received rejections, especially when they were new at the business of writing.)

My life course had been chartered, I wrote it down on paper, and I was not going to change it; therefore, I did the next best thing (maybe crazy!): I started a publishing company.

I knew absolutely nothing about the publishing business and I spent months reading books, talking with book printers, publishers, distributors, and so on. I really worked hard. You have to remember that while all this work was going on, I had a full-time job, was teaching, and doing volunteer work. (I bet you can see the halo on my head!)

The book was published and very slowly it started

selling. I was able to sell enough to cover the costs and have enough money to print the next book. This is my fifth book and I am barely breaking even. That is O.K., I truly love writing and I have learned so much. (I know there is still so much more to learn and that excites me.)

There are four more books in the making, two of which will be written by other people.

4. Down size your business – keep only the clients you feel good about.

This was really scary! I was aiming toward financial instability. I used to worry when there was nothing to worry about: am I looking for a nervous breakdown? Is this what I really want? How could I be contemplating 'throwing out of the window' what I had worked so hard for.

I worked and reworked budgets. If I lost one client I would have so much less money, if I lost two clients I would have so much less money. What if the computer broke? What if the roof leaked, what if, what if..

I would say a prayer, then a 'what if', one more prayer then one more 'what if'. I realized that my faith and trust in God were being taken over by my insecurities and slowly, very slowly I started feeling comfortable again. I would have less, but the less would be more than enough.

Colleagues are hassling to keep current clients and finding new ones, and me? I want fewer clients? Am I really that crazy? Sure, why not!

Over a period of three years I was able to 'lose' some accounts, mostly those who made enjoying my business difficult. I also closed my outside office and moved the business in my home.

I remember when I started in this business. The first year I did work out of my home and I could not wait to have an office outside. I had to have an office outside; that meant I had achieved some type of respect and credibility.

I had had an outside office where I was paying rent for twenty years, and when I finally was completely honest with myself, I realized that it was not out of need but for appearance. The office in my home is equally professional and certainly less expensive. In addition, it allows for so much flexibility and freedom.

Today I still have a viable business. Clients do not mind coming to my house, actually, they feel more relaxed and, although the business is smaller, my mortgage gets paid every month.

During this period I have also realized that material things are not as important as spiritual things. Feeling good has become very important to me. In addition, the realization that I cannot take things with me when I die certainly has helped my cause.

5. Keep teaching, but teach what you like also, like Italian.

I love to teach. I absolutely love to teach. Put me in front of a whole bunch of students and see me sparkle! Well, the sparkle was getting smaller, teaching the same business courses over and over again for a couple of decades, got to be somewhat UN-sparkly!

Over the last few years I had the opportunity to tutor a few people on learning the Italian language (I speak 'perfetto' Italian) and I liked it very much. Not only it was ideal to retaining the command of my native language, but it also was bringing me back to my roots. So, I started teaching Italian at cultural centers and other institutions. I loved it and it gave me the brilliant idea to write a book! So I did, I wrote a book on learning the Italian language together with a one-hour audio cassette.

My plan now is to teach a limited number of business courses and put more emphasis on teaching Italian. I plan to keep on teaching Italian for a few more years before I will write another, much more extensive Italian book, probably a full-fledged textbook.

My life is so exciting, so diverse. I have enough plans to keep me busy until I am 100!

6. Thank God every day for everything you have.

How could I not thank God? Everything I have I owe it to Him. Everything I am I owe it to Him.

For so long I searched for spirituality and always looked in the wrong places. Now I am able to look back and truly see that through the course of my life God was always with me and He presented me with choices all along. I made the choices. I chose the material world over the spiritual world. I have come to realize that although I treated God as the enemy, over and over again, He never abandoned me; He was always at my side ready to help me, if I ever acquired the wisdom to look inside my heart.

As I told you before, all through my life I was searching for spirituality and it was there for the taking! God truly presented me with the opportunity to find spirituality and I never pursued it, I never chose the way of the heart. Indeed, when I look back, I can see He offered the opportunity for spirituality to me, 'on a silver platter' and I turned my back on Him.

What things happens to people, how they happen, and why they happen are a mystery, part of His plan and I cannot question such plans. I have been able to understand, over the last few years, why certain things happened to me in the past, things that when they happened caused me to be baffled. I now know there is a purpose to everything.

When I look back I see that God treated me with 'kids' gloves', He truly held me in the palm of His hand.

I have been spared from so many bad things, bad things that happen every day to people: illnesses, deaths, accidents, poverty, and the like. It is as if was sheltered by Him; perhaps, it is because He knew what a weakling I was. I hope it is also because He knew one day I would come to my senses.

I am now a much stronger person. My mother is not in good health, actually, her health is very poor. I doubt she will be alive much longer. The thought of her death saddens me for I shall miss her dearly. I know I am not afraid of what will be, it is part and parcel of life. I will accept her death when it comes and I believe she will be in the company of God. I also believe she will be watching over me all day and all night, always. I find much comfort and peace in that.

I do thank God everyday. My heart and my mind are as one; I mean it and I feel it.

If you think I am in the process of becoming a 'perfect' human being, think again! I am prone to failure, to weaknesses of character. I do make mistakes on a regular basis (that is something I can count on!); however, the need to do good, to be good, and to do His will is becoming stronger. I am able to understand better and faster when my will, not His, is trying to run the show. This is when invariably I fail and make mistakes.

I fall down and He picks me up.

How could I not thank God?

I want to tell you another story now.

I gave a garage sale last year. Oops, I have to tell you something else before the story.

I started having garage sales, two per year, a few years ago. Prior to that it used to be 'beneath' me to have a garage sale. Number one, my things were too good to be sold at a garage sale. Number two, people might have thought I had a garage sale because I needed money. Number three, I did not want 'those' people on my property! Was I messed up or what?

At this garage sale came an older woman, probably about seventy years old. She was dressed very shabbily and I noticed that her left shoe had a hole from which part of the little toe was out. There appeared to be a very large corn on that small toe. She limped a bit when she walked. Her face was very thin, almost skinny, and it was filled with deep wrinkles. Her hands looked rough and unkempt as if those hands never felt hand cream on them.

Her eyes were nice and had honesty in them. I don't know the exact color of her eyes, somewhere between light green and light blue.

She drove a very old and very run down car. The original color must have been white but, between the rust and the dust, it was hard to tell.

She greeted me with a shy smile and asked me if she could look around. She made the rounds of the garage a few times. I saw her lift the teddy bear and almost pressing it to her chest. Three times she stopped by the bear. Some other people came in, bought something, and left. She still was looking. Then with her back at me I saw her take her wallet out of her 'falling apart' purse (the wallet was in bad shape too) and count her money. She then put her wallet back in her purse a perused some more. Once more she went by the teddy bear and caressed its face. While this was going on I took all but ten dollars in singles out of the moneybox and went to her. I asked her if she could hold the moneybox while I went to the bathroom. She really looked at me as if I had asked her to hold the 'crown jewels.' She was very hesitant, almost in fear. I told her I would only be gone for one minute.

When I came back I saw her clutching her hands on the money box ever to tightly.

She stayed for a few more minutes and then she bought a pair of kitchen curtains for one dollar. I asked her about the teddy bear, how I saw her looking at it; maybe she wanted to get it for her grandchildren? She said that she did not have any grandchildren and she did not need it. I gave her the teddy bear and before I could say anything, she stepped back and said: "No, I don't want it, I cannot buy it." I handled it to her and I told her it was hers, it would not cost her anything. I told her it was a thank you for minding the 'store' while I went to the bathroom.

You could not have believed the expression on her face: surprise, astonishment, happiness. Those eyes sparkled! She took it real fast, as a child would, and again pressed it against her chest. I told her not to thank me but instead to say a prayer for me. She left with the teddy bear pressed against her chest.

For the next few months, until the cold season came, I would find spiritual cards in my mailbox. About six times I found flowers outside my garage as I was leaving for work. The stems of the flowers would be inside a plastic bag, half filled with water and closed up with twine.

Once, about six in the morning, I heard the rattle of an old car outside my window. I did not look out, I knew who it was. I knew it was the old lady, and I found it very comforting.

I gave her an old teddy bear, and she brought me
God.

Chapter 8: MY KITTIES

I hope you like cats, but if you don't, pretend I am talking about dogs or whatever pets you like.

I have seven cats of all ages, and at one time I had as many as ten. I tell you, to keep after them and keep the house clean was becoming a full time job!

I only have stray cats and cats that were on 'death row'. Of the seven, three were abused kittens. Although they are now adults, from their behavior I believe they still have not forgotten the abuse.

Cats remind me of me: so fearful and fragile and at the same time so fearless and independent. Most of all they remind me of me because their behavior can be just plain 'nutty'. I love them and they love me.

Occasionally it is so hilarious when two or three of them want to be on my lap – all at the same time!

They sleep with me and sometimes I can't even move or turn. The worst part is that when I try to move or turn I am afraid of disturbing them!

No wonder they think I am their pet!

I hope you have pets. They bring comfort and companionship and, most of all they need to be loved. They too are His creatures.

Chapter 9: BOOTSIE

God works in mysterious ways, it is true.

It is also true that He works in marvelous ways.

When the heart is like that of a child and it listens to Him, wonderful things can happen.

The scenario: That day I did not feel very cheerful, actually I felt rather miserable. Somehow I was feeling sorry for myself because I never had become a mother; I never had a child. I had the 'poor me' attitude and thought this was rather unfair. This is what happened.

A lady who feeds stray cats and dogs (she is an angel!) had found this little kitten right in the middle of a street. She took him to a vet and from the vet she called me. She explained that the vet did not want to keep the kitty there. The vet said the kitty was too sick and he should not be amongst the other animals.

She asked me if I could keep kitty for a couple of days. I agreed and I went to pick up the kitty.

He looked absolutely terrible: he was so skinny

that one could see all the ribs through the fur. He had such a bad respiratory infection that with every breath he omitted horrible sounds. The vet suggested that he be put to sleep as he did not have a chance to survive; he was too sick and had gone without food for too long.

I was unsure what to do until the kitty looked at me. It was as if he was begging me to rescue him.

The poor baby did not know how to eat and did not know what food was. I put some kitten food on a plate and he did not touch it. The noise from the infection was so terrible that I had resigned myself to have a dead kitty in the morning.

He was so skinny I was afraid to hold him that I might hurt him. I started putting just a bit of food in his mouth and he spit it out. This went on for a while until, finally, he swallowed it. In total, after about two hours, he had eaten the equivalent of a teaspoon of cat food.

The kitty had ear mites and fleas to boot.

I spent a total of three hours with the kitty that evening, trying to feed him, moistening his lips with water, giving him medication, and holding and caressing him very gently. I even sang to him.

When I went to bed I had a hard time falling asleep as the thought of finding the kitty dead in the morning was so saddening. I already loved that little baby.

The morning came and I rushed to his room. He was alive!, barely. He had not touched the food at all during the night so I fed him again. This time he did not spit the food out. His infection appeared to be even worse and it tore my heart in half to listen to him breath.

I took him to the water bowl and again wetted his lips. I gave him the medication, and gently started cleaning his ears with a moist tissue. I told him I loved him.

In the week that followed he had to be taken to the vet three times for shots and other medication. The vet still thought kitty should be put to sleep.

Two weeks went by and that morning, when I went to his room, a miracle unfolded: he had eaten almost one half can of food, drank some water, and used the litter box. As I opened the door he came towards me purring so divinely.

This is Bootsie, this is the baby God had sent me.

It was quite a while later that I understood what happened, what God had done for me. God made me feel and behave as a mother would. How very young did I feel!

Bootsie is very healthy today and very mischievous too!

Chapter 9: CONTENT

Am I content? Most of the time yes. I am not when I have a loss of memory: when I forget how beautiful my life really is. I have everything and much, much more. My health is good and I understand how terribly important that is.

What good does it do to have the fancy car, the beautiful villa, etc., etc. when you are dying of cancer?

My friend Larry was a successful attorney. He had all the material things he wanted. He worked very hard for them, often resulting in depriving himself to be with his family. They found the cancer and the best medical treatment did not save him. He was dead within one year.

In this last year of his life we often talked about life. Though he felt good about all he accomplished in life he realized that he had missed out on life. He told me it was as if he was seeing his family for the first time. Such a beautiful family and he cheated himself out of their love and of sharing life with them. He started noticing nature as if he had never seen it before.

One day when I went to visit him at his home, he was sitting on the grass holding a rose. He had tears in his eyes. He looked at me with the saddest eyes I had ever seen and he asked me: 'Why? Why didn't I ever see the beauty of a rose before? Do you know that this rose smells better than the most expensive perfume there is? Do you know that my family is more beautiful than this rose? What have I done to them and to me?' He sobbed, almost out of control. I was mortified, I did not know what to say. I hugged him and cried with him. I talked to him and told him about the goodness of God.

I know I talked for a long time but I do not remember most of what I told him.

His last few months transformed him into a most beautiful human being. He spent all his time with his family, with nature, in prayer, and in doing good deeds. What a most spiritual power of example he has become for me!

My health has been good, except for minor aches and pains. Last week I went to the doctor because my left knee was bothering me. He told me: "Nothing to worry about, it is just the process of aging..." I stopped him right away: "What do you mean by 'aging'"? "A little girl like me!" He laughed but I could tell he thought I was a bit weird. Oh, well.

Yes, I am content. I wake up in the morning and I feel happy because I have another day. Another chance to appreciate the beauty around me. I look at the trees and I look at the flowers and I find them so very beautiful.

Have you ever hugged a tree? I mean hugged a tree with love? Try it and feel God loving you back.

Working in the business world can be trying when you want to keep spirituality in your heart, but it can be done, I know, because I can do it. I should say that NOW I can do it. It was not always like that; actually, it was much easier to be negative than to be positive. Slowly, the change came, and when I say 'slowly' I mean it has taken years. Because I have been filled with character defects all my life, at times I do not do what I preach; however, now I am able to quite readily determine that I 'goofed' and rectify my mistakes.

There are a few rules I try to live by:

1. I don't complain about my job. How fortunate I am to have a job. It means I have the

knowledge and experience to do something useful. I always try to do a good job and do it efficiently. That brings me pride and contentment.

2. Sometimes when I am tempted to think about my clients/coworkers as bad and/or unfair I stop and I instead pray for them. I smile at them, and it is a real smile. I try to see the little girl/boy in her/him.

   Have I ever walked in their shoes?

3. The work is hard/tiring? Would it be easier if I were sick at home or in hospital? Would it be easier if I were in the unemployment line?
   I want to learn and work willingly.

4. I need to do the very best I can. I cannot compare, judge, and criticize. If I feel an urge to judge and criticize I look into the mirror (did you get this?)
   I need to remember who the REAL boss is!

5. I say the Serenity Prayer:

   God, Grant me the serenity to accept the things I cannot change,
   Courage to change the things I can, and
   The wisdom to know the difference.

The above rules can easily be modified to fit any situations.

Also, I am learning to answer this question before I act: What would God do? I fully realize that I cannot reach perfection, or even be very good at something; however, I have the willingness to do the best I can do and be the best I can be.

Chapter 11: YES, I AM FIFTY

My mother called me last week to wish me a Happy Birthday.

I asked her: "Mom, do you realize that I am fifty? Do you know that I have lived one half century? Am I old?"

This is her answer: "Number one you are my baby, number two you are beautiful, number three if you don't die you will get even older, and number four I am seventy five years old and if I don't complain it means you better shut up!"

How about that? I guess I didn't get any sympathy.

I told her I really was not complaining about it, it just seemed to be strange that I was fifty. She told me what I knew she would tell me: "You are as old as you want to feel."

I knew that! And now I also know that there are two ages: the biological age (that's the one that stinks!) which changes the physical appearance and the strength of the body, and the soul age, the age that allows an older body to be happy and free as a child.

At the 'young' age of forty-eight I sat on Santa's lap for the first time! (I know what you are thinking!) It was a wonderful experience – after it was over.

Going to sit on the lap of Santa Claus is one thing that all children are entitled to and every child wants to do. I had never sat on Santa's lap and I wanted to experience it.

I got in line behind a 'pack' of screaming happy children and their mothers. Sooner than I thought I started getting weird looks from the mothers.

The mother right in front of me asked me if I was going to see Santa by myself, without any children. I told her yes, that I had never done that before, and just now I was fulfilling that childhood wish. She told me that she understood and that she wished she had the courage to do the same thing. I told her she did not need courage, just less self-centeredness. I asked her if deep inside she was still a child. She did not answer but I am quite sure I saw tears forming in her eyes.

So, I went to sit on Santa's lap – just a bit embarrassed. I was fully aware of the eyes looking at me, and I was even trying to imagine what the people were thinking.

You see, I am self-centered too.

I talk a good talk, but I fail too.

As I started to sit on Santa's lap (he really looked like Santa Claus! – including the belly) he started laughing and told me I made his day! He asked me what I wanted and I told him that what I wanted was to sit on Santa's lap, so I already got what I wanted.

I told him I would pray for him and his family that God be with them at Christmas and always. He thanked me and then he said: "God bless you".

Because I also like to have the last word, I told him: "I am, and I have been for forty eight years."

By the way, I did have my picture taken with Santa Claus.

Yes, that was a nice experience. I did fulfill a childhood wish and now I had something less to feel sorry about!

Lately I have been doing quite a few things that even five years ago I would have never thought about doing, something as simple as picking wild flowers in a park or watching the sunset by the lake.

There are so many, so many things that can be done to keep in touch with God and to keep feeling young. I feel so very young inside and it seems that with feeling young I also feel a sense of purity and of joy that I truly have never experienced before.

For many years, I was what I thought people wanted me to be. I dressed, spoke, and behaved as I thought I should, to 'fit in'.

I know you probably believe that I turned into a Pollyanna, but you are wrong.

I am fully aware that life is life, quite unpredictable. The saying 'Life is not a bowl of cherries' is not accurate. Life IS a bowl of cherries: I love cherries but cherries have pits and it can really hurt if I bite into a pit. So, I try to get the best out of life and carefully discard the rest.

Things happen every day, good and bad. Just turn on the television set during the news or read the daily paper. Some things are so bad they defy comprehension.

We actually do get a distorted view of life though, because bad news is reported much more than the good news. Good news does not sell as many papers or find as many television sponsors as bad news does.

I do agree that this does not make too much sense, but I do not try to analyze it or understand it anymore. I have one life to live and I want to make the most of it by living it with good things and goodness.

For many years I lived with fears: fear of abandonment, fear of loneliness, fear of financial hardship, fear of being rejected.

In a way, I think that trying to be what I thought I should be caused those fears, those insecurities.

I do not exaggerate when I say that I never have been this 'young'. I am so free, I am who I think I should be and I behave accordingly.

Do you know that I pick pennies up from the street? I would never pick up a nickel or a dime, or even a quarter (I would not want people to think I needed money!), but I do pick up pennies. Why? 'Pennies from heaven? In a way, yes. Pennies, like stray cats do not appear to be worth that much. They are ignored and at times viewed as a burden.

Take care of the little things and He will take care of you.

I do something else. (Have you ever met anyone this weird?) For every penny I pick up I give five dollars away. I know that the math does not work here, but this is true: I pick up one penny, I give five dollars away, and then I find out that I am five dollars and one penny richer than I was before!

It took a long time to come to this point, and I do realize that I could not have been here sooner because I was not ready. I had to stop, carefully review my life, plan for my life, and live my life.
I have found my place in life. It is a simple life and an exiting life. I had to reach deep inside my heart, and open it to God so that He could work wonders for me.

God allowed me to see my life, the life I so often complained about as a child. He opened my eyes to the beauty that was there and I could not see.

God as allowed me to be the child and the woman I want to be.

Chapter 12: BE YOUNG!

There is nothing that can be done to stop biological aging: next year I will be fifty-one either I like it or not. The only things I can do is to take good care of my body and (there is absolutely nothing wrong with it) to try to look as young as possible. (No, I do not go around wearing mini-skirts or a ponytail.)

Just because my age gets to be in the 'high digits' does not mean I have to seat in a rocking chair waiting for the end to come.

God has given me life and I know He wants me to live it, which brings me to the 'soul age'.

I want to and I need to feel young. I told you before that I don't go around wearing mini-skirts or ponytail; what I mean is that like a child I want to feel the innocence and the purity. If I have a choice to think good or to think bad I will choose good.

Do you think that going to sit on Santa's lap I did something childish? I tell you: no, I did not! To be rather honest, I think adults belong on Santa's lap more than the children do. We adults know what

Christmas is about, not about toys, but about a miracle that has allowed us to live life and to choose how to live it. We always had that choice: how to live life.

Do you know that when today becomes yesterday it will never comeback again?

When I look at yesterday I want to be able to say: "It was a good day, I am grateful and I do not have regrets about it. Today I also want to have a good day.

The only way I know to have a good day is not by what is around me, but by behaving and reacting to it in the best possible way I can.

To have a good day means to keep my heart as pure as I can and to remember that He is at my side.

So, what do you think? Who are you? Are you happy? Are you afraid of 'old age'? If we are lucky enough, we will see old age.

Do not be afraid of getting older but of feeling old.

Take care of your body and more importantly, take care of your soul.

It does not matter what your life circumstances, you can always feel better and younger.

You know, everyday I go to work. By the time I leave the house I will have spent a couple of hours feeding the cats; cleaning their litter boxes; dusting and straightening up; checking my e-mail; washing and beautifying myself; scheduling things to do after work; deciding if I have enough food in the house to have dinner, and more.

My workday may go well or it might not. The people I come in contact with may be in a good mood or they might not.

What I am trying to say is that I can keep my spirituality and a youthful outlook for life regardless of what happens.

You see, the first thing I do when I awake, after thanking God for allowing me to awake, is to ask Him to be by my side as the day unfolds. As I go through the day I behave and do things with the knowledge that He is right beside me. Everything appears easier and better with Him at my side.

The circle of life: how absolutely mysterious and fascinating it is!

IT IS LIFE! And life can be quite beautiful.

Do not waste time. Become young!

Start smiling more. Smile especially at those people you encounter who appear to be sad or troubled.

Carry small toys with you to give to the child who is crying.

Help that lady load the groceries in the car.

Let the mother with the child, or that old man or woman ahead of you at the checkout counter.

Tell your friend and your family how fortunate you are to have them in your life.

Don't wait till Christmas to give a good tip to the newspaper delivery boy or girl. Surprise them with a tip and a card thanking them for the good service.

Spend five minutes each day to remember good times.

Spend five minutes each day listening to God.

Ask God to come along with you, make Him your trusted companion.

If you like, write to me. Get the mailing address and the e-mail address at the end of the book. I would like to hear from you and I promise to get back to you right away.

I want to leave you with a final thought on how to keep young.

When the time comes for my body to cease to exist I want to be able to say:

I have experienced life to the fullest.

I have been young forever.

I have found the innocence, hope, and love that were lost somewhere in life.

I have found the greatest love, God, and I have tried to do His will.

With the heart of a child I have allowed God to set the course of my life and I have NO REGRETS.

May God hold you in the palm of His hand, always.

PROLOGUE

As I put the finishing touches on this book I hear the terrible news about John F. Kennedy Jr., his wife, and his sister in law. The plane on the bottom of the sea has not been found yet.

Dear God, your will be done.

Dear God, may the gratitude in my heart never diminish.

Dear God, keep my heart simple, keep me young for the rest of my life.

SOME PICTURES.....

Me and my friend in the background.

I still miss her so much.

In life I try to follow your example, my friend.

Italy, my home town.

Such a pretty country ... so far away ...

Mother is there.

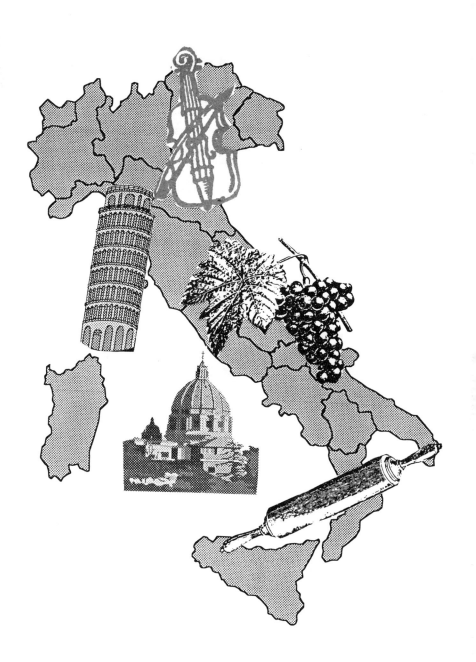

That skirt: I still don't remember. I just tried it on again ... I think it shrank some more.

These are hand-crocheted napkin holders.

You know who made them, don't you?
(It wasn't me!)

Me ...   Sixteen going on sixty-one!

My prized possession!

What a beautiful reminder of perseverance, hope, and willingness.

My hometown: Carrara.

This picture does not do it justice.

I blamed this lovely and peaceful town for my miseries ... so unfair was I.

So much sorrow in your eyes, mom.

Father had just passed away ... the worst was yet to come.

Forgive me for my selfishness, for my ignorance.

Father, daddy. I love you. Did you like my poem?

I know you and God are watching over me, I feel safe.

My babies! A whole bunch of them!

Will they ever learn that I am supposed to be the 'boss'?

Bootsie .... My beautiful baby!

Never again will I doubt the goodness of my God.

Mailing address:

Elvira Bellegoni
ETTA Publishing Company
28605 Lakeshore Blvd.
Willowick, Ohio 44095

e-mail address:

elvira.bellegoni@mailcity.com

Our books can be purchased directly from ETTA Publishing Company or through the major Internet retailers, including Amazon.com.

When you order from us please include $2.50 for shipping charges. If you order more than one book, add $2.50 for one book plus 75 cents for each additional book. Please use the attached order form.

Elvira would be happy to sign your book. Write on a piece of paper what you want her to write. (Note: this can be done only if you purchase directly from us.)

Please send your order to:

ETTA Publishing Company/50
28605 Lakeshore Blvd.
Willowick, Ohio 44095

ORDER FORM

Name of Book_____

Price per book _____X quantity ordered ___=_____
Shipping   _____

TOTAL   _____

Dedication: _____

_____

_____

**Make check payable to ETTA Publishing Company
and mail to:**

**ETTA Publishing Company
28605 Lakeshore Blvd.
Willowick, Ohio 44095**

ORDER FORM

Name of Book_____

Price per book _____X quantity ordered ___=_____
Shipping   _____

TOTAL   _____

Dedication: _____

_____

_____

**Make check payable to ETTA Publishing Company
and mail to:**

ETTA Publishing Company
28605 Lakeshore Blvd.
Willowick, Ohio 44095